I0796091

This gift is for:

____

Who is deeply loved by:

____

May you have power . . . to understand Christ's love.
May you know how wide and long and high and deep it is.

—*Ephesians 3:18 NIrV*

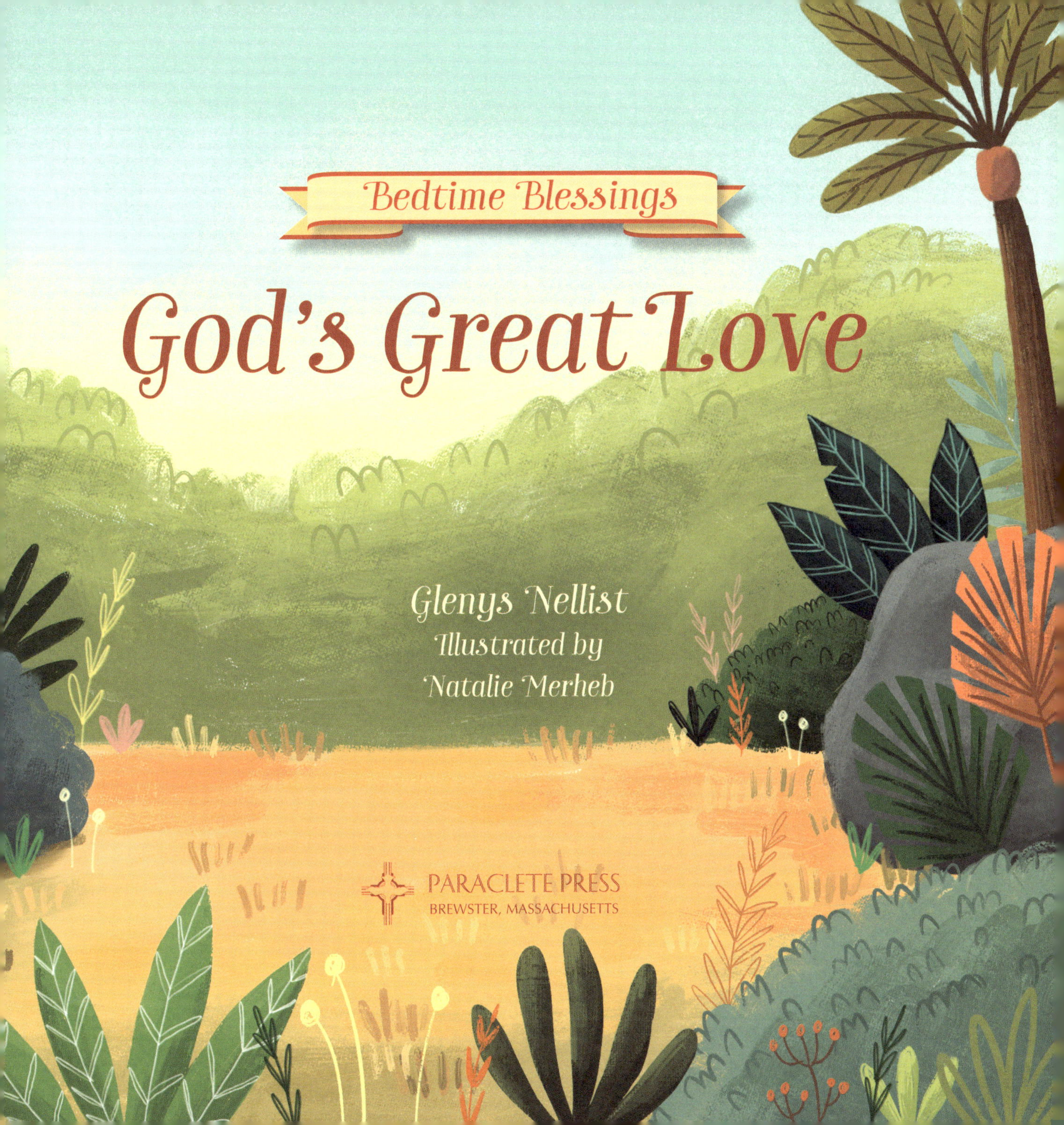

Bedtime Blessings

God's Great Love

Glenys Nellist
Illustrated by
Natalie Merheb

PARACLETE PRESS
BREWSTER, MASSACHUSETTS

Little One, I pray for you,
As you lie down to sleep,

That you will know God's love for you,
So high and wide and deep.

God's love for you is taller
Than the tallest, tallest trees.

It's higher than a kite
Pirouetting in the breeze.

Far higher than the mountains
Or an airplane up above,

Much higher than a rainbow
Is God's amazing love.

It's longer than the river
That disappears from view,

Much longer than a hiking trail
Is God's great love for you.

It's wider than the oceans
That stretch from shore to shore,

It's broader than the painted skies—
God couldn't love you more!

Far deeper than the deepest sea
Where dolphins dive through blue,

Far grander than a canyon
Is God's great love for you.

And there is nothing . . . *nothing*
That could take God's love away.

God will always love you,
Every minute—night or day.

So as the nighttime closes in
And stars begin to shine,

Imagine God sings over you,
"I love you. You are mine."

Little One, I pray for you,
As you drift off to sleep,

That you will know God's love for you,
So high and wide and deep.

There is power in speaking blessings over your child. After you finish reading this book to your little one, gently trace the shape of a cross or a heart on their forehead (or palm) as you say a blessing over them. If your child is awake, look into their eyes. Fill in your child's name in the spaces below and use any of the following blessings:

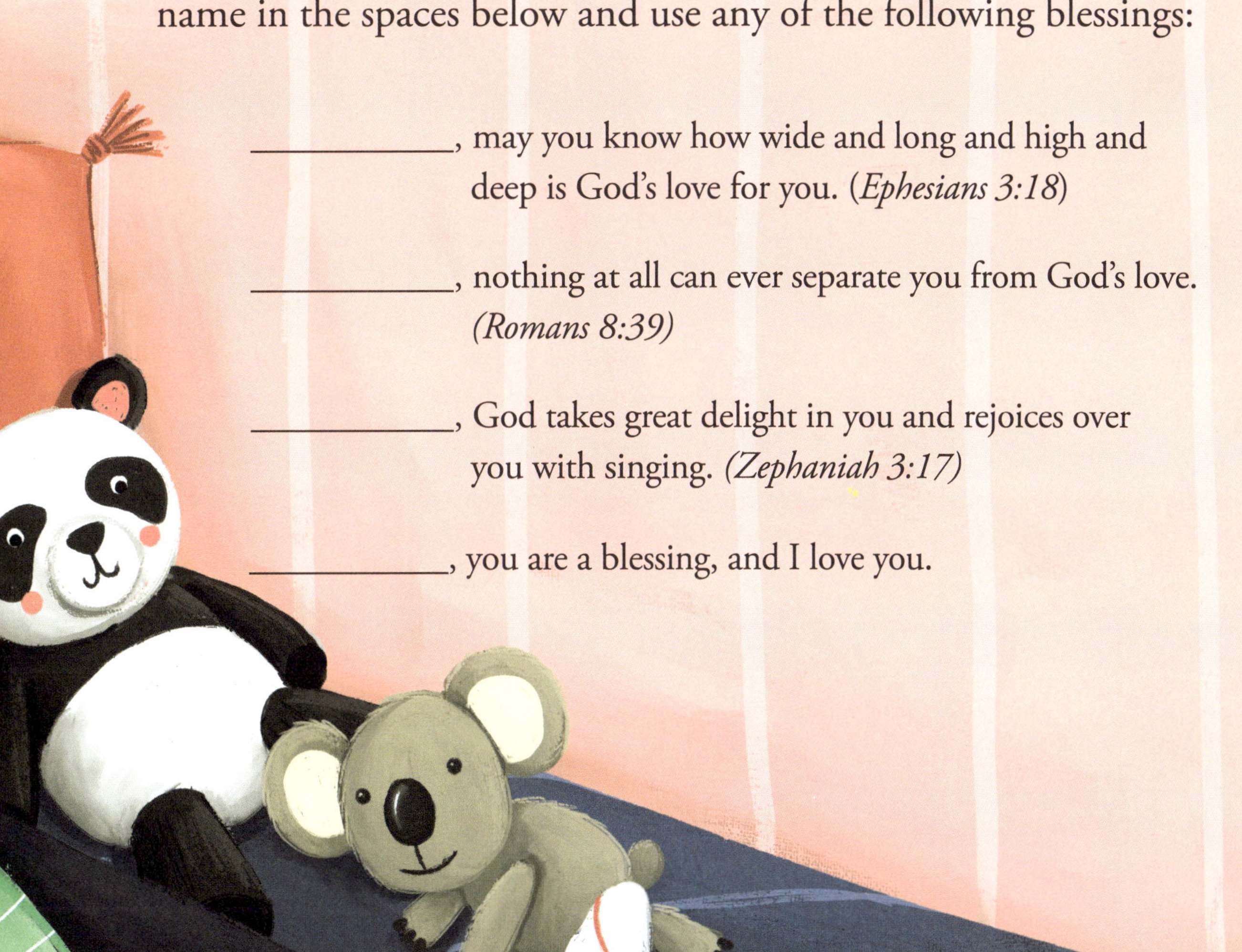

____________, may you know how wide and long and high and deep is God's love for you. (*Ephesians 3:18*)

____________, nothing at all can ever separate you from God's love. *(Romans 8:39)*

____________, God takes great delight in you and rejoices over you with singing. *(Zephaniah 3:17)*

____________, you are a blessing, and I love you.

Glenys Nellist is a bestselling author of many children's books, including five popular series: *Love Letters from God*, *Snuggle Time*, *'Twas*, *Bedtime Blessings*, and *Little Mole*. A former teacher, Glenys has a passion for bringing the Bible to life and speaks in schools and churches. She and her husband are proud parents of four adult children and happy grandparents of four little ones.

Natalie Merheb spends her time illustrating nature, animals, and recreations of classics. She lives in Dubai with her husband and twin daughters. When she's not illustrating, you'll find Natalie horseback riding in the desert, trying new recipes, or relaxing on the beach with her family.

2025 First Printing
Bedtime Blessings: God's Great Love

ISBN 978-1-64060-941-9

Library of Congress Control Number: 2025932652
10 9 8 7 6 5 4 3 2 1

Published by Paraclete Press
Brewster, Massachusetts
www.paracletepress.com
Manufactured by RR DONNELLEY (GUANGDONG PRINTING SOLUTIONS CO.,LTD.
Printed June 2025 in Dongguan, Guangdong, China
This product conforms to all applicable CPSIA standards.
Batch: 20250630GPSL

Also available: